W9-AAV-730

Raves for John Guaspari's
I Know It When I See It

"Anyone who reads it without coming to a significant—almost gut level—understanding of what quality really is ought to get a one-minute reprimand."

> KENNETH BLANCHARD
> CO-AUTHOR OF *THE ONE-MINUTE MANAGER*

"After you've read all the other prayerbooks of the major quality religions and can't seem to find true faith, pick up and read this book. The light will go on."

> DAVID L. DOTLICH, EXECUTIVE VP
> BULL HN INFORMATION SYSTEMS

"I loved this great little book because it was fun to read and it made me think. What more can you ask?"

> STEW LEONARD, OWNER AND CHAIRMAN
> STEW LEONARD'S DAIRY STORE

"Customer service and quality are what we serve, (and) John's book has gone a long way towards focusing the Garden staff on its off-the-ice and off-court performance."

> LAWRENCE C. MOULTER
> PRESIDENT AND CHAIRMAN
> NEW BOSTON GARDEN CORPORATION

"Both *I Know It When I See It* and *The Customer Connection* are valuable resources that we use to spread the quality message. John Guaspari takes an intangible concept and explains how quality service *can* be managed. . . . The simple yet powerful message is meaningful to all."

> EMILY PENTECOST
> MANAGER OF QUALITY ASSURANCE
> OPRYLAND HOTEL

Other AMACOM Books by John Guaspari.

I KNOW IT WHEN I SEE IT
(also available in paperback)

THE CUSTOMER CONNECTION:
QUALITY FOR THE REST OF US
(also available in paperback)

THEORY WHY: IN WHICH THE BOSS
SOLVES THE RIDDLE OF QUALITY

John Guaspari's ideas on quality are available on videocassette. For more
information about this video and John Guaspari's other award-winning,
best-selling videos—QUALITY IN THE OFFICE; WHY QUALITY?;
THE QUALITY CONNECTION; and I KNOW IT WHEN I SEE IT—
please call the AMA Video Customer Service Center at 800-225-3215
(in Mass., call 617-926-4600) or write to them at 9 Galen Street,
Watertown, MA 02172.

IT'S ABOUT TIME

A Fable About the Next Dimension of Quality

John Guaspari

Author of *I KNOW IT WHEN I SEE IT*

amacom
American Management Association

New York • Alanta • Boston • Chicago • Kansas City • San Francisco • Washington, D.C.
Brussels • Toronto • Mexico

This publication is designed to provide accurate and authoritative
information in regard to the subject covered. It is sold with the
understanding that the publisher is not engaged in rendering legal,
accounting, or other professional service. If legal advice or other expert
assistance is required, the services of a competent professional person
should be sought.

Library of Congress Cataloging-in-Publication Data

Guaspari, John.
    It's about time: a fable about the next dimension of quality/
John Guaspari.
        p.   cm.
    ISBN 0-8144-5130-6
    1. Total quality management—Miscellanea. I. Title. II. Title:
It's about time.
HD62.15.G83 1992   92-17963
658.'62—dc20   CIP

Design & illustrations: DESIGN PLUS, Koehli/LeBrun

Printing number

10 9 8 7 6 5 4 3 2 1

For
Antoinette and **Harry,**
who always found time

Acknowledgments

To all of my Rath & Strong colleagues, I say thank you. They are an energetic and energizing group of people, and I treasure my three years among them.

Some specific thank-yous to, in alphabetical order, Meredith Allen, Dave Berlew, and Dan Ciampa for insightful critiques of early drafts that made this a better book.

Ed Hay is to time as The Boss is to punctuation marks. For his expertise and his willingness to share it with me, I am most grateful.

It was a pleasure to work with Myles Thompson throughout the conceptualizing, drafting, and polishing of this book. AMACOM is well served by him.

Were my wife, Gail, my son, Mike, and my daughter, Joanna, not the center of my world, I wouldn't acknowledge them here. But they are, and I have.

Finally, I'd like to acknowledge my basset hound, Ernie, who's as lovable as they come even though he's a bit of a pinhead.

John Guaspari
Walpole, MA

PROLOGUE

Even skeptics of old say *the* issue today

Making all other issues retreat and give way

Is an issue so basic it's even been said

That some books on the topic have even been *read!*

It's your Quality that will determine your fate

So that yesterday's good is today's second-rate.

To ignore it can make corporate leadership blanch.

It just must be addressed or you won't have a chance.

Men like Deming and Crosby and Dr. Juran,

Each can get you results like those made in Japan.

Such terrific results that to you they'll accord

Presidential congrats or a Baldrige Award.

Every day we're all seeking the Quality edge,

Leaving no stone unturned, leaving no bet unhedged.

Looking this way and that, every chance we'll exhaust,

Every option explored to cut Quality's cost.

Doing all of the things that it's said we must do,

But if everyone does them, just where's that leave you?

Any edge held by all is an edge held by none.

Can an edge be an edge if it serves everyone?

Knowing what, knowing how, knowing when, knowing why:

Wouldn't everyone know? Wouldn't everyone tie?

All these questions point out an abiding concern.

Recognize that it's there, one more lesson to learn:

Do you know what comes next, after quality's "done"?

Should you sharpen your focus, or is the game won?

ONE

Once upon a time there was a company called Punctuation, Inc., which made (invented, as a matter of fact) the punctuation marks that we use in day-to-day writing and discourse to make things logical and clear and keep them from becoming an overlappingconvolutedgrammarbustingjumbledupmess.

Their story is a simple one, a happy one, and by now a pretty well-known one.

In a nutshell—and with the help of Punctuation, Inc.'s Bullet line of specialty punctuation marks—that story can be summarized thusly:

- Punctuation, Inc., had dominated its markets for years.

- Process, Inc., a new competitor, appeared on the scene and began to take market share away.

- Punctuation, Inc., ignored Process, Inc., at first, saying: "We've had challenges before. We always come out on top. The competition always goes away."

- This time, though, they didn't go away, and The Boss began to take the threat seriously. When he asked customers why they were taking their business to Process, Inc., they said, "Quality." And when he asked them to be more specific about Quality, all they could tell him was, "I know it when I see it."

- This was frustrating for The Boss. Because when he looked at Punctuation, Inc.'s Quality records, he saw that things were within tolerance, on spec, on the money. Except that the customers' money was being put on Process, Inc.

Well, The Boss (and his associates at Punctuation, Inc.) did such a good job of solving the mystery—just what was the "it" customers knew when they saw?—that Punctuation, Inc., had become world renowned as *the* place to go if you wanted to know about Quality. Punctuation, Inc.'s story was a compelling one, and the use of its Quality punctuation marks in the telling of the story made it all the more incisive and insightful.

So incisive and insightful, in fact, that the world couldn't get enough of it. Reporters were constantly calling on The Boss to hear his latest musings on matters Quality.

The Boss kind of minded and kind of didn't.

On the one hand (as his right-hand-man often reminded him), "This publicity is great, but we've got a business to run. Taking our eye off the ball is how we got in trouble in the first place."

On the other hand (as his left-hand-man would always counter), "You've been named Quality Man of the Year for six years in a row. You have an obligation to give something back. And besides which, the publicity is good for business!"

Invariably The Boss would do the interview or offer the advice or make the speech. As, in fact, he was doing right now, telling the by-now-he-would-have-thought-universally-familiar-but-apparently-not Punctuation, Inc., story to three members of the press who had gathered in his office.

"We thought we were doing a good job of Quality," he told them, "but we were wrong. Almost dead wrong."

The reporter for the tabloid *Gazette* scribbled away in his notepad. At the end of every line of notes he affixed an exclamation point from Punctuation, Inc.'s Feisty line of products.

"It wasn't until we turned around and looked at Quality from the customer's perspective that we got things right."

The reporter from the *Daily Journal*, the broadsheet newspaper of record, wrote her notes in complete paragraphs, full of lengthy sentences and complex clauses set off by Punctuation Inc.'s Respectable line of products.

"Once we figured that out, we were back on track. It's ironic. Our problems came from not listening to our customers. And yet so did our solution, because they finally screamed loud enough for us to hear. Thank goodness they did."

The TV reporter perked up at this. Although the interview had lasted for more than an hour, she hadn't taken a single note. But now she took out her Sound Biter, an accessory made by Punctuation, Inc., for the electronic media market, and grabbed The Boss's statement right out of the air.

The right-hand-man signaled that the interview ought to be wrapped up. The Boss caught the sign.

"Thank you, ladies and gentlemen, but I'm afraid we have to wrap things up. I'm visiting a new customer in an hour, and I want to be prepared."

"Thank you," said the reporter from the *Daily Journal*, respectably.

"Many thanks," intoned the TV reporter in blow-dried tones. "Now back to you!"

"Yeah, thanks!" exclaimed the reporter from the *Gazette*.

As the left-hand-man ushered The Boss's guests out the door, the *Gazette* reporter asked one last (feisty) question: "Send me a copy of your company's annual report, will ya?"

"Certainly," said The Boss. Turning to his left-hand-man he added, "Please make a note of that and take care of it."

"Sure thing," said the left-hand-man. This is what he wrote in his notebook:

(ANNUAL REPORT TO *GAZETTE*

He stopped writing and began patting his pockets, searching for something. He looked in his briefcase. He looked in his notebook. He looked through his file for the meeting.

"Problem?" asked the right-hand-man.

"Yes," said the left-hand-man. "I seem to have run out of close parentheses. I need one to make a note of his request."

The right-hand-man started patting his pockets and looking through his notebook and briefcase.

Ditto The Boss.

Ditto the reporters from the *Gazette* and the TV station.

But they all came up empty.

"Uh," said the *Daily Journal* reporter, "maybe you could use one of these."

At that she handed the left-hand-man something that looked like this:

(

"But that's an open parenthesis. I said I needed a close parenthesis," said the left-hand-man.

"Flip it over," the reporter said. "Now what do you have?"

"Well, I'll be . . . ," the left-hand-man muttered as he fixed the object to his notes, which now read:

(ANNUAL REPORT TO *GAZETTE*)

"Pretty clever," added the right-hand-man. "You turn it around and it becomes something completely different."

"Where did you get that?" asked The Boss.

The *Daily Journal* reporter flushed. "I ordered it. It's called a PAIRenthesis. It came from a new company called EMIT, Inc. I think they're called that because they've been putting out products left and right. They say they're going to turn things around in the punctuation marks business."

NEW COMPETITOR ATTACKS PUNCTUATION, INC.!! is what the *Gazette* reporter wrote in his notebook.

"Somebody new on the scene to help keep us in fighting trim? I welcome the competition!" boasted the right-hand-man.

"Yeah," agreed the left-hand-man. "There's just one thing I have to say about that: It's about time!"

The newscaster's Sound Biter snatched the left-hand-man's "It's about time!" comment out of the air.

The Boss took it all in, put on a brave face, showed a confident front.

But he was feeling a familiar feeling, and it worried him.

In the weeks and months that followed, EMIT, Inc., kept emitting new products and innovative services.

- Iridescent exclamation points called Lookouts to be used on warning signs near steep cliffs, high voltage, and any number of carnivorous hazards.

- Moisture-resistant marks called Gurglers to be used by infants. (These came with little detachable training wheels.)

- A Talk Now, Pay Later financing plan for customers with a solid credit history. (Charter subscribers were also given a free lifetime supply of EMIT, Inc., decimal points and dollar signs to use when writing payment checks for this service.)

All of which had The Boss concerned. He was sitting at his desk. On it were a PAIRenthesis, a Lookout, a Gurgler, and a Talk Now, Pay Later application form.

The Gurgler (a comma) had its training wheels attached. The Boss wheeled it back and forth across his desk and smiled at the creativity it symbolized. Slowly, the smile dissolved into a frown.

There was no escaping it. EMIT, Inc., represented a competitive threat not to be taken lightly.

Just then the right-hand-man and left-hand-man entered his office for their daily what's-up meeting. They were talking excitedly, animatedly. Obviously, something good had happened, and The Boss was eager to hear about it.

"What's up?" he asked.

The left-hand-man answered. "We just got the latest results from our Customer Satisfaction Tracking Survey. Our ratings are higher than ever!"

The right-hand-man chimed in. "That didn't happen by accident. It correlates exactly with the improvement efforts we've put into place over the past eighteen months."

"I never cease to be amazed at how right you've been about all this Quality stuff," said the left-hand-man.

"Yes," added the right-hand-man. "You've said all along that Quality was the key." He waved the Customer Satisfaction report in the air. "And our customers are telling us just how right you've been."

The Boss said, "Good, I'm glad to hear it." But his expression said something else, and the left-hand-man and right-hand-man could see the difference.

They asked The Boss, in unison, "What's the matter?"

Gesturing to the EMIT, Inc., products on his desk, The Boss answered them with a question: "What did our customers have to say about these?"

The right-hand-man responded, "These are all new products. Our survey began six months ago, so they're not included."

"Oh, I see," said The Boss. "Because these products weren't around six months ago, we shouldn't be bothered by them today. And because it takes us six months to take a reading, these products don't count. Heard any trees falling in any forests lately?"

The left-hand-man didn't like the trajectory of this conversation. He tried to deflect things onto a more positive course. Pulling out the latest Quality report, he proudly proclaimed, "The defect rates on every one of our products dropped significantly during the past quarter. We're down to twenty parts per million. And falling!"

The Boss could tell his message hadn't gotten through. "As far as I can see," he quietly pointed out, "we've *never* had a defect on a PAIRenthesis, or a Lookout, or a Gurgler, or a Talk Now, Pay Later contract."

There was a pause as the right-hand-man and left-hand-man exchanged confused glances. "But we've never offered those products," explained the left-hand-man.

"I guess that's a pretty sure-fire way to keep our defect rates at zero. And to make sure we never get any customer complaints about them," responded The Boss with deepening sarcasm.

The right-hand-man and left-hand-man were concerned. They knew they were being dressed down, and that was bad enough. But beyond that, they had been through a lot with The Boss, and they were concerned about him.

"We're a good company, an excellent company," pinged the right-hand-man.

"We're in the middle of a record breaking year," ponged the left-hand-man.

"We've won the International Quality Award each year since its inception."

"You've been named Quality Man of the Year for the past six years."

"Competitors have come and gone!"

"We've got the best and the brightest people!"

"Absenteeism is down!"

"Productivity is up!"

"Labor-management unrest is over!"

"Job dissatisfaction is out!"

The Boss sat and listened, unfailingly polite, increasingly concerned. Because as the right-hand-man and left-hand-man continued composing their congratulatory couplets, it became clearer and clearer to him that, despite all they'd done over the past six years, they still didn't get it.

When the right-hand-man and left-hand-man finally ran out of steam, The Boss spoke. Even though he was frustrated at what he had seen and heard in this meeting, his tone was unemotional, measured, and businesslike.

"If we're so good, if we're such a Total Quality company, then we ought to be able to come up with a Quality response to what these represent," he said, pointing to the EMIT, Inc., products on his desk.

Though the right-hand-man and left-hand-man weren't 100 percent certain of what to do once they left this meeting, there was no doubt about what to do right now.

"OK, Boss," is what the left-hand-man said.

"We'll get right on it," is what the right-hand-man said.

"Thank you," is what The Boss said.

It's about time is what The Boss thought.

THREE

Three weeks had passed since The Boss had given the left-hand-man and right-hand-man the charge to do something about the competitive threat from EMIT, Inc.

During that time, The Boss had been concerned and impatient. The right-hand-man and left-hand-man, on the other hands, had been business-as-usual and, as far as The Boss was concerned, disconcertingly serene.

During that time, EMIT, Inc., hadn't been concerned, impatient, business-as-usual, or serene. They had, instead, been busy, using the time to bring out new products and services:

- A Green Line of fully recycled (and recyclable) punctuation.

- CompuMarks, pixelated marks used on the screens of personal computers.

- A 1-800-EMIT INC telephone line for technical assistance, application ideas, and late-breaking news in the world of punctuation. (The line was initially established to provide a focal point and clearinghouse for information regarding the infamous Serial Comma Killer that plagued word processing programs nationwide. Since that threat had passed, EMIT, Inc., was able to quickly transform the toll-free number into a customer service offering.)

Obviously, much had been happening, at least at EMIT, Inc.

The Boss was eager to find out what had been happening at Punctuation, Inc. Because he was a modern manager, The Boss had empowered, enabled, inspired, and facilitated the left-hand-man's and right-hand-man's ability to respond to his request. Because he was only human, such a hands-off approach drove him crazy. But his anxiety was about to be alleviated.

It was Friday afternoon, 2:58 P.M., and he was just two minutes away from a meeting in which the right-hand-man and left-hand-man would present their action plan on how to deal with EMIT, Inc.

The Boss reread the ad for the three new EMIT, Inc., offerings and grimaced. Just then, the right-hand-man and left-hand-man appeared in his doorway.

"Is it time for our meeting?" they asked.

"High time," answered The Boss. He couldn't help but let his eagerness show. "What have you got for me?"

"We think you'll like what we've got to say," said the left-hand-man.

"Yes," added the right-hand-man, "we now think we understand what has been going on with EMIT, Inc., and we have developed a plan to deal with them."

The left-hand-man jumped in. "This plan has been three weeks in the making. And although not-wanting-to-hide-our-lights-under-a-bushel-wise, we think we have done a good, thorough job, the plan represents the hard work of many, many people."

"There were the people in manufacturing," chimed in the right-hand-man, "in HR, in accounting."

"Don't forget R&D and marketing," added the left-hand-man.

"Of course not," said the right-hand-man. "And we'd be remiss if we didn't acknowledge the contribution of the folks in the communications department who made the quality slides I'll be using."

"*And* the attractive hard copies!" beamed the left-hand-man.

"But of *course!*" alphonsed the right-hand-man.

"*Au certain!*" gastoned the left-hand-man.

"Get on with it!" bossed The Boss.

The right-hand-man and left-hand-man were first shocked, then hurt, by the outburst. The Boss moved to make amends. "I'm sorry," he soothed. "Both of you. I'm delighted to hear about the participation of all of our associates. But this EMIT, Inc., business has been a cause for great concern, and I'm most eager to hear what you and your colleagues have come up with. Please proceed."

The left-hand-man spoke first. "First of all, it would seem as though EMIT, Inc., has managed to attract a very high-caliber, creative work force. How else can you account for breakthroughs like the PAIRenthesis, Lookouts, Gurglers, and the Talk Now, Pay Later plan?"

The Boss showed them the magazine ad for EMIT's even newer breakthroughs.

"Precisely my point!" continued the left-hand-man. "Our approach will be to out-recruit them. We'll get the best, brightest, most creative talent that's out there."

"To ensure that's done in a Quality way," added the right-hand-man, "we will develop a finely tuned recruiting and hiring process. Clearly and precisely defining suitability criteria for candidates. Putting them through a painstaking interviewing process. Pooling inputs and driving for consensus to preserve the unique Punctuation, Inc., culture."

"Sounds good, sensible," said The Boss. "When do you figure you'll have this up and running?"

"Oh," said the left-hand-man, glancing at the right-hand-man, "eighteen to twenty-four months?"

The right-hand-man nodded, adding, "Give or take."

"Isn't that kind of a long time?" asked The Boss.

"People are our most valuable asset," said the right-hand-man. "We have to spend the time to ensure Quality in the process."

"Remember," said the left-hand-man, "it took millions of years and constant pressure to make diamonds. Back to the time when dinosaurs roamed the earth!"

The Boss wasn't sure why, but dinosaur imagery didn't ease his concerns.

"Anyway," continued the left-hand-man, warming to his task, "once we have those folks on board, we will also have a finely tuned New Product Development—NPD—process in place, with the emphasis on the word 'process.' The checkpoints will be built in to make sure their work doesn't go astray. Clearly delineated review and approval authority will help us ensure that we take advantage of the collective wisdom and expertise contained inside these walls."

"Will that take another eighteen to twenty-four months?" asked The Boss.

"Oh, of course not," said the right-hand-man, laughing. "We develop the NPD process in parallel with our recruiting efforts. Of course, as far as the new product development itself goes, it's anybody's guess. A year, maybe two to get a prototype out. Then there's alpha testing, beta testing. But, hey, Rome wasn't built in a day!"

The Boss wasn't sure why, but imagery of another Italian city, Pompeii, flashed through his mind.

"We saved the best for last," said the left-hand-man. "The only reason that EMIT, Inc., has been able to develop all of these new and moderately interesting products is that they're small enough to be pretty fast on their feet. And there's our edge."

"Because of our size," added the right-hand-man, "we can run higher-volume production. Bigger batches. That increases our capacity utilization and brings our unit costs down."

"We can move up the learning curve faster," said the left-hand-man, "giving us an even bigger cost advantage."

"And," continued the right-hand-man, "we have the leverage to get volume discounts from our suppliers. Which drives our costs down further still."

"It's ultimately about costs," concluded the left-hand-man, "and that's how we'll beat them. That, of course, and Quality. That's why it's important for us to take the time to do it right. It's an investment in designing the Quality in, and who knows more about Quality than us? We've got the record to prove it!"

The Boss knew that what they said made good, orthodox, business sense:

>hiring the best people . . .
>
>managing the process . . .
>
>economies of scale . . .

moving up the learning curve . . .

volume discounts . . .

designing the Quality in.

He heard himself telling the right-hand-man and left-hand-man that they had done a very good, thorough job. He heard himself telling them to put the plan into action, to "get right on it." He heard himself thanking them again and saw himself shaking their hands as he ushered them from his office.

But he was concerned, and he wasn't sure why.

The Boss went to his window and stared out. It was a sunny, albeit breezy, day. An airplane flew by in the distance, and white smoke began trailing behind it. Skywriting.

The Boss watched as the message took shape:

Tired of the same old, same old?

You and 1,000,000 of your fellow

citizens of our fair town. If you

want a new recreational treat that

can't be beat, come on out to the

! theme park where everything's

exciting!

"That," thought The Boss, "is the longest sky-writing message I've ever seen."

And the most amazing thing was, it didn't move. Despite the high winds.

Five minutes passed. Ten minutes. Fifteen minutes. The Boss stared. The message remained, locked onto the sky.

Then the airplane came back and erased the message. Swoop, swoop, swipe, swipe. And it was gone.

An idea occurred to The Boss. He went to his phone and dialed 1-800-364-8462. 1-800-EMIT INC.

"For new product information, touch 2," said the disembodied voice.

The Boss, nervously, did so.

When he did, this is what he heard:

"Be on the lookout for high-flying advertise-ments for EMIT, Inc.'s new theme park: *!* (The Boss wasn't sure how they communicated *!* over the phone, but they had somehow pulled it off.) "EMIT, Inc., has developed a new skywriting capability—SKYLOCK—that renders the old 'now you see it, now you don't' problems of skywriting obsolete."

The Boss was stunned. With one phone call,

TIRED OF THE SAME OLD.

YOU AND 1,000,000 OF

CITIZENS OF OUR FAIR

WANT A NEW RECREATIONAL

CAN'T BE BEAT, COME ON

! THEME PARK WHERE

two new EMIT, Inc., capabilities had landed on his already sagging shoulders: a theme park and the SKYLOCK technology.

"Thanks for calling 1-800-EMIT INC for the latest in product developments. Have a nice day."

The Boss wasn't having a nice day at all. He looked at his watch. It was 6:00 P.M. It had been a long day, a long three weeks, and the weeks ahead were giving every promise of being considerably longer.

He hung up the phone and gathered up his papers, briefcase, and car keys. Switching the lights off as he left his office, he allowed himself one consoling thought. "At least the weekend's here. At least now I can relax a little . . . put EMIT, Inc., out of my mind."

A final pause, a final thought: It's about time.

FOUR

It wasn't just any weekend for The Boss. It was the one weekend of the summer that his son, daughter-in-law, and (truth be told, the part that made things really special for The Boss) his two grandchildren came to visit for the holiday.

The Boss's son was a successful businessperson. (He ran a company that made the little bits of lint, dust, scraps of paper, loose change, and other odds and ends that you find in the pockets of trousers that have not been worn for several months.)

His daughter-in-law was an even more successful businessperson. (She ran a consulting service—Flashing 12, Inc.—for people who didn't know how to program their VCRs. Business was booming.)

His two grandchildren were terribly successful

at being, well, good little kids. (Although even The Boss would concede to a raging case of grandparental myopia on this score.)

The Boss and his son were sitting on the deck, which overlooked The Boss's backyard, which overlooked a meadow, which overlooked a scenic lake, which underlooked The Boss's comfortable but not overly ostentatious home.

It was early Sunday evening. They were having a predinner cocktail, and The Boss was feeling a bit sentimental.

"It's really great to have you here," The Boss said. He smiled as he looked through the sliding glass door and saw his grandchildren terrorizing his family room.

"It's great to be here," answered The Boss's son. "I'm just sorry we can't be here more often. But with our schedules, there just never seems to be enough time."

"No need to apologize. I wasn't exactly the perfect host, spending all day yesterday working in my study."

"Just like old times," reminisced The Boss's son. "That's how I remember you on weekends. Working in your study."

"If only we had it to do over again, maybe it'd be different," mused The Boss.

"Nope," said his son, categorically. "Can't be. Life moves at a certain pace, and it's speeding up all the time, and you've got to get on board or you get left at the station."

"My, but aren't we getting philosophical in our old age," kidded The Boss. His son smiled, a tad embarrassed. "But I'm afraid you're right. If somebody could find a way to bottle time . . ."

"I'd like to bottle the time we had at that theme park yesterday!" offered The Boss's son, changing the subject. "It was great. What do they call that place again?"

"!," said The Boss (somehow).

"Catchy name. Sorry you couldn't be with us."

The Boss shrugged a whattyagonnado shrug. "Duty calls," he said.

"Well," said The Boss's son, "at least Congress finally got around to declaring Malcom Baldrige's birthday a national holiday so we can spend a long weekend with you."

The Boss smiled and held up his glass. "To Quality," he offered.

(31)

"To Quality," his son responded.

"Dinner is served!" announced his wife.

"It's about time!" shouted his grandchildren in a way that, coming from them, passed for charming.

Dinner went well beyond charming all the way to sensational. And it wasn't just the food. What was so sensational was the overall event, the overall dining process. The way everyone worked together and pitched in with the cooking (although The Boss's wife was most assuredly "the boss" in this department), setting the table, cleaning up spills (small children were, after all, present), clearing the table, washing the dishes, gliding smoothly into the living room for after-dinner liqueurs.

The conversation and the kidding.

The laughing and the loving.

The carefree creativity of the kids.

It was all very special, a very special time, which, as is the wont of special times, passed most quickly.

"Good times go by fast, bad times hang around much longer," mused The Boss. "If we could figure out a way to turn those times around, we'd be on to something."

The Boss had no idea just how right he was.

FIVE

Later that night, as they were getting ready for bed, The Boss picked up the brochure from *!* that his wife had put on her dresser.

"You know what I wish?" he asked.

"No, dear. What?" responded The Boss's wife.

"I wish that somehow we could capture just a fraction of what we had here tonight and infuse it at work."

"Now, dear. You have a fine company. You're always worrying when you should be appreciating."

"I know, I know. But the dinner. Everything about it. It was like a finely tuned machine. It was like, like . . . it was like clockwork!" He glanced again at the *!* brochure, and his thoughts flashed to his meeting of two days ago with his right-hand-man and his left-hand-man. "If my company had been responsible for this dinner, everyone would have worked very hard, and we'd have wound up doing a great job, a Quality job, but I have this nagging fear that it would have taken us too long to get to that point. We're so caught up with Quality—making sure we 'Do it right the first time!'—that we'd have spent three months doing feasibility studies on the salad dressing."

"Well," she consoled him, "you're at home now, and tomorrow's a holiday. Get a good night's sleep. You'll have plenty of time to think about those things on Tuesday."

"I guess you're right," he responded. Although deep down, he wasn't so sure.

"Good night."

"Good night."

And another day had passed.

Or so he thought.

Bzzzzz!

It was 7:00 A.M., and his alarm clock was commanding The Boss to arise.

"Mmmrrfff," he mumbled to no one in particular as he slapped the alarm off, rolled out of bed, shuffled into his bathroom, and tried to remember just when they had gotten an alarm clock with a buzzer that buzzed instead of a bell that rang.

It was early, certainly earlier than he normally got up on holidays. But the kids would be leaving today, and he had already missed the trip Saturday to !, and he wanted to spend as much time with them as possible. So he trundled on downstairs (shaving and showering could wait) into the kitchen.

"Morning, Grandpa!" said The Boss's granddaughter and grandson, seated at the kitchen table.

"Morning, Dad," said The Boss's son and daughter-in-law, tableside too.

"Morning, dear," said The Boss's wife. She seemed a bit distracted by some sort of paperwork on the kitchen counter in front of her.

"Mornin' all!" boomed The Boss, as he took his place at the table (in between, naturally, his two grandkids).

"What would you like for breakfast, dear?" asked The Boss's wife.

"Oh, I dunno," he answered. "Orange juice, corn flakes with bananas, wheat toast, coffee, I guess."

The Boss's wife wrote all this down, which struck The Boss as being odd, seeing as how it was the same breakfast he'd had every morning for the past thirty-seven years. But he let it pass, as his grandson was tugging at his sleeve.

"Grandpa! Will you play a game with us?"

"Yeah!" chimed in his little sister. "It's called Kitty Kat, Kitty Kat. We maded it up ourselves!"

"Yeah!" said her brother. "Ourselves!"

And as he said this, he waved his arms in front of him and—*presto!*—a cat appeared, suspended in the air above the kitchen table.

At that, The Boss's son looked up, sharply, from his newspaper.

Seeing this, The Boss's son's son waved his arms again, and—*poof!*—the cat disappeared.

But it was too late. The damage had been done.

The Boss's son turned to his wife. "Did you see that?" he asked, clearly annoyed.

"Yes, I did," she said, equally annoyed.

What the——? thought The Boss, in minor shock at the sight of the feline apparition.

"Just what makes you kids think you can just make up and play a game called Kitty Kat, Kitty Kat?" The Boss's son asked his children. "Making cats hover over the table! Have you been authorized to do so? Have you  taken it through the review process?"

"No, Dad," said The Boss's grandson.

"Have you submitted a written proposal for our consideration?" asked The Boss's daughter-in-law.

"No, Mom," said The Boss's granddaughter.

"They're just kids," The Boss said to his son. "Playing. Being creative."

But The Boss's son made it clear that *he* was *not* playing: "I'll thank you not to undermine my authority, Dad. Yes, it's just kids playing. But I think the kids' mother and I have something to offer in terms of steering them in the right direction so they'll get the most benefit out of that playing. We were kids once ourselves, you know. A little time spent upfront ensuring the Quality of their recreational activities is time well spent."

"Now," said The Boss's daughter-in-law to her daughter, "if you kids get working on it now, you can have your proposal to us by the end of the day."

"Yes, Mom," said The Boss's granddaughter.

"We can read it over and discuss it when we get home tonight," added The Boss's son, "and get you our inputs within seventy-two hours."

"Yes, Dad," said The Boss's grandson.

"Before you know it," smiled The Boss's son, "you kids will be playing Kitty Kat, Kitty Kat—or a reasonable approximation thereof. How's that?"

"Good," said the kids, although their faces didn't believe their ears. (Neither, quite frankly, did The Boss believe his. It had been a long time since he had small children, but it seemed to him that if you have to use the word "thereof" to a child under ten, you probably haven't handled things as well as you could have.)

Mercifully, the doorbell rang.

"Who could that be at this hour?" The Boss asked, heading to the door.

"Probably the teaspoon cleaner," answered his wife, matter-of-factly.

"The what?" asked The Boss.

"The teaspoon cleaner," came the one-sixteenth exasperated reply.

"I thought that's what you said," said The Boss, over his shoulder, as he reached the back door.

And, sure enough, it was the teaspoon cleaner. At least it was if the gleaming, six-foot teaspoon attached to the roof of his van and the identical-in-every-way-but-size teaspoon stitched above the breast pocket of the man-who-had-rung-the-doorbell's coveralls was any indication.

"Good morning, sir," the man greeted The Boss. "Teaspoon Express, at your service!"

"Uh, yeah, uh . . . come right in," stammered The Boss.

And the man did, heading straight for the kitchen sink. Picking out the teaspoons and only the teaspoons—not soupspoons, not butter knives, not juice glasses, not frying pans, not cereal bowls, not forks, just teaspoons—he went to work.

And truth be told, he did his job brilliantly, which also describes how the teaspoons shined when he was done with them. Then he stood aside, waiting, waiting, waiting, until another teaspoon needed cleaning, which he then did with dispatch.

As he headed back to the kitchen table, The Boss whispered to his daughter-in-law, "Isn't that kind of odd? Why do we need a service like that?"

She gave him a look that redirected the word "odd." "We use the same service. Have for years!"

"But what about all the stuff he's not cleaning? How's that going to get done?"

"Haven't you ever heard of Soupspoon Express? Butter Knife Express? Coffee Cup Express? Saucer Express?"

"Yeah, I guess," lied The Boss. "But all those services must be expensive. And look at him—standing around waiting for teaspoons when he could be cleaning something else."

His daughter-in-law shook her head. "If you want a Quality job, you get the best, brightest, most creative, most specialized talent out there. It might cost a little more and take a little longer, but that's the price you have to pay for Quality. After all, isn't that why we're here today celebrating Baldrige Day?"

"I guess so," said The Boss. And while he wasn't exactly lying, he knew that he at least felt kind of funny about all this. It all seemed kind of . . . surreal.

Most of all, though, he felt hungry. But when he sat back down at his place, he found what looked for all the world to be a form letter:

Dear *Dear*:
Thank you for your
recent breakfast order.
We regret to inform
you that the following
items are on back order:

CORN FLAKES
BANANAS

We will deliver these
items just as soon as
they are available.
We are sorry for any
inconvenience this
might have caused you.

"What's this all about?" The Boss asked his wife, holding the letter aloft.

"I'm sorry dear, but your breakfast is on back order. We're running French toast this week."

"What do you mean 'running French toast'?"

"I mean that's all I'm making this week."

"But not everybody's having French toast," he said, gesturing to the other plates around the table. (As he did so, he accidentally knocked a butter knife onto the floor. The Teaspoon Express guy ran over, bent down, saw what it was—and left it, returning to where he had been standing.)

"I know, dear. I got those out of finished goods inventory."

"From where?" The Boss asked.

"You know," answered his wife. She walked to the window and opened the blinds. "From here."

The Boss couldn't believe what he was seeing. Or, to be more precise, what he *wasn't* seeing. Because instead of seeing the lake out his kitchen window, he saw what looked for all the world like a warehouse, with forklifts and shelves and bins and refrigeration units and all the rest.

"What's that?" The Boss asked in amazement.

"Why, that's our warehouse and our forklifts and our shelves and our bins and our refrigeration units and all the rest," his wife answered.

"What do we need with all of that?" The Boss demanded.

"Why, we need that to make sure we can meet demand. Of course, a fat lot of good that did you

this morning." Everyone laughed, except The Boss.

"Grandma," called The Boss's wife's granddaughter. "My English muffin doesn't taste right!"

The little girl's mother picked up her daughter's muffin, took a bite, and spoke to her mother-in-law. "She's right, Mom. It's overcooked."

The Boss's wife's face said oh-dear. "I have no idea what could have happened. According to my production schedule, those were made"—she checked the paperwork on the counter—"over a month ago. Lord knows how we're going to trace the cause of the problem. The trail's pretty cold by now. In the meantime, we'd better run some more muffins to pick up the slack." Turning to her husband, she added, "And I'll make a note to bump up the volume the next time we run corn flakes and bananas, too. Which will be in"—she checked a chart on the kitchen wall—"three weeks."

"But why can't you just make that breakfast today?" The Boss asked.

Now it was his wife's turn to be exasperated. "Honestly, dear. For someone who runs a business, sometimes I wonder about you.

"By running just French toast I can be more efficient and productive . . . move up the learning curve faster . . . realize economies of scale . . . keep utilization up . . . secure volume discounts, which is why it's a good thing we have our warehouse.

"And look how the line is set up: eggs, bread, butter, milk, maple syrup, cinnamon, fry pan, spatula. Like clockwork!

"If I had to make French toast and then scrambled eggs and then corn flakes and bananas, why—"

"Setups would kill efficiency," said her grandson.

"Utilization would drop through the floor," added her granddaughter.

"Exactly!" said The Boss's wife, delighted.

"Terrific!" said The Boss's daughter-in-law, delighted.

"Fantastic!" said The Boss's son, delighted.

"Excuse me," said The Boss, light-headed.

"*Hhhwackkk!*" hhhwackkked the disembodied cat, as a fur ball poofed into view and hovered over the table. A quick flick of The Boss's son's son's wrist and the fur ball poofed out of sight.

The Boss got up from the table, saying, "I think I need to lie down."

He put his coffee cup in the sink (seconds later, the teaspoon gleamed), gave his wife a peck on the cheek, and headed upstairs.

When he got to his room he pulled the covers up and lay on his back. The last hour, he thought, had been bizarre. But at least now he could relax. Now he could unwind. Now he could reenergize the way he was supposed to be able to reenergize on a holiday.

"It's about time . . ." was as much as he could think before he slid off to sleep.

Or so he thought.

"Dear, dear . . . it's time to get up," said The Boss's wife, gently shaking him awake.

"Mmmrrff," The Boss replied.

But his wife persisted. "Come on, come on. It's after seven o'clock."

The fog lifted from The Boss's brain. "After seven o'clock!" he shouted, bolting up. "You let me sleep until seven o'clock at night?"

"Of course not," his wife assured him. "It's after seven in the *morning*, and everyone's waiting for you to come down for breakfast. You were sleeping so soundly, you slept right through the alarm bell."

Seven in the morning? Breakfast? Alarm bell, not buzzer? Could it be?

Only one way to find out, The Boss thought.

"I'll be down right after I shave," he said to his wife. "Just one thing, though."

"What's that, dear?" she asked.

"I don't want French toast. I *must* have corn flakes and bananas for breakfast!"

She gave him a puzzled look. "What makes you think you'd have to have French toast? And of course you can have corn flakes and bananas. You've only had that for breakfast every morning for thirty-seven years. There's no need to get nasty about it."

The Boss needed to make amends. "Sorry, sorry. Didn't mean to snap. Just woke up . . . not thinking straight . . . ragtime . . . you understand."

"I guess so," she said, giving him the benefit of several doubts and heading back down to the kitchen.

The Boss called to her in the hallway.

"Dear?"

"Yes?"

"One more thing?"

"Yes??" Her good nature was wearing a bit thin.

"Is the teaspoon guy still around?"

"Excuse me? What teaspoon guy?"

"Never mind, never mind," The Boss replied. "Just more ragtime. Sorry."

"OK, I guess," laughed his wife, only marginally concerned about his sanity.

So it was all just a dream, thought The Boss. The French toast, the Teaspoon Express, the Kitty Kat, Kitty Kat review board.

But where had it come from? What had been on his mind lately to cause such a dream?

He *had* been thinking a lot about work, especially about his Friday meeting with his right-hand-man and left-hand-man.

And he *had* been thinking—obsessing might be more like it—about EMIT, Inc.

Almost subconsciously he picked up the *!* brochure from the dresser and carried it into the bathroom with him. Standing before the mirror, about to shave, he took a long look at the brochure.

! on the cover. EMIT, Inc., logo on the back. Attractive design, he thought. And a formidable foe. But at least we've finally got a plan in place to deal with them. "It's about time," he said softly to himself. "It's about time."

He looked up at the reflection in the mirror: His unshaved face, and the back cover of the brochure, on which, since it was a mirror image, the EMIT logo looked like

TIMƎ

And all at once it hit him.

"It's about *time!*" he shouted out loud.

Loud enough, in fact, to be heard by the others in the kitchen.

"Don't worry," The Boss's wife told her family. "He just woke up."

"Oh," said her granddaughter. "Ragtime."

"Yeah," added her grandson, looking at his sister and nodding. "Ragtime."

And upstairs The Boss repeated to himself, with less volume but no less enthusiasm, "It's about *time!*"

SEVEN

The Boss was excited. So excited, in fact, that he double-timed it from the parking lot to the Punctuation, Inc., headquarters building.

"Good morning!" said a number of Punctuation, Inc., employees to The Boss as he passed them in the hall.

"It's about *time!*" The Boss responded to each of them, all of whom were a bit confused by this response but more than a bit impressed by The Boss's energy and all-around get-up-and-go-ness following a long holiday weekend.

Barely had he deposited his briefcase on the floor behind his desk, taken off his jacket, and rolled up his sleeves, ready for a good day's work, when his right-hand-man and left-hand-man appeared in the doorway.

"I was just going to call you!" he beamed, motioning them to take a seat at his small conference table. "I gave your plan for dealing with EMIT, Inc., a lot of thought over the weekend, and there's one phrase that best sums up where my thinking is on it: It's about *time!*"

Now it was the right-hand-man's and left-hand-man's turn to beam. (It is for moments like this that right-hand-men and left-hand-men live.)

"Therefore," The Boss continued, "we won't be following your plan."

At that, the right-hand-man and left-hand-man stopped beaming.

"Excuse me?" gulped the right-hand-man.

"Gulp," added the left-hand-man. "I'm a bit confused. You thought about the issue, and you thought about our plan, and you thought, *It's about time?*"

"That's right," said The Boss, happily.

"So *therefore* we won't be following the plan?" asked the right-hand-man.

"Exactly!" answered The Boss.

"You don't mean, 'In spite of the eminent good sense your plan makes, we won't be employing it'?"

asked the right-hand-man.

"Or, 'Although the ideas you have come up with redefine the boundaries of enlightened management as we approach the new millennium, I have a new paradigm I'd like to test out'?" queried the left-hand-man.

"You mean, 'It's about time—*therefore* we won't be following your plan'?" asked both the right-hand-man and left-hand-man.

"Now you've got it," said The Boss.

But from the looks on their faces it was clear to The Boss that, whatever they had, they didn't realize they had it, and whatever they knew, they didn't know they knew it.

"Let me take a moment to explain," said The Boss, kindly. "We won't get anywhere if I cause you two heart failure.

"Question: what's the purpose of our business? What do we make here?"

"Money?" offered the left-hand-man.

"Too cold. Not enough heart," replied The Boss.

"An enriching workplace environment?" tried the right-hand-man.

"Too warm. Not enough grit," replied The Boss. "What we make here is customers. And we'd better keep making them and keeping them or we won't have a business."

The right-hand-man and left-hand-man nodded. What The Boss said was difficult to dispute. But where was he taking them?

The Boss leaned forward in his chair, compelling the right-hand-man and left-hand-man to do likewise. "What's the most valuable commodity customers—*people*—have today?

> the thing there's never enough of . . .
>
> the thing they aren't making any more of . . .
>
> the thing you don't get a second chance at . . .
>
> the thing that when it's gone—*pfffttt*—it's gone?"

The right-hand-man and left-hand-man sat and thought. And then they sat some more and thought some more. They recognized this as the sort of prove-your-mettle moment that it was and wanted to be sure to get it right, so they sat and thought some more still.

A minute passed.

Then two.

Then three.

It was, all in all, quite uncomfortable. Finally, the left-hand-man spoke up. "We appreciate your giving us a chance to voice our ideas. But why don't you just tell us? We've got other things to cover, and time is short."

"Never mind us," added the right-hand-man. "I'm concerned about the use of *your* time. You haven't got all day, and time's a-wastin'."

"It's about time you guys figured it out!" The Boss declared, giving them each a congratulatory handshake.

"Figured it out?" asked the left-hand-man.

"Figured what out?" asked the right-hand-man.

"It's about time you figured out that it's about time!" explained The Boss. "Time is the issue. That's how EMIT, Inc., is beating us. It's about *time!*

"It's not that they're doing things better than we are, it's that they're doing them *faster!* And since time is what's of most value to customers, then faster is quite an advantage. Faster *is* better."

"Ohhh!" said the right-hand-man, slapping his forehead in recognition. "I see what you're saying!"

"Ahhh!" added the left-hand-man, experiencing his own flat-forehead moment. "I hear you now!"

The right-hand-man stood up and walked over to the in-box on The Boss's desk.

"It's always good to go back to the basics, like in-box exercises," he said, straightening up the papers in the in-box and giving them hospital corners. "Our training department offers an excellent time management course. We can put everyone through it"—he caught The Boss's slight frown—"as a refresher in your case, of course."

The left-hand-man warmed to the theme. He tapped The Boss's pocket calendar, which was on the table in front of him. "You're so right. Betcha there's a fair amount of unproductive stuff in here"—The Boss's slight frown got a little less slight, which was not unnoticed by the left-hand-man—"but not nearly as much as in mine!" he recovered.

It was beginning to dawn on the right-hand-man and the left-hand-man that they still didn't get it. Their expressions weren't completely crestfallen, but certainly a lot crestlower than when they had been beaming.

The last thing The Boss wanted was for his right-hand-man and left-hand-man to be discouraged. "Look at it this way," he explained. "Punctuation, Inc., has twenty-four times sixty times sixty seconds each day. How many is that?"

The right-hand-man and left-hand-man whipped out their calculators. When confused, they liked good, clear, tasky stuff to do. And this was stuff at its taskiest.

"86,400!" shouted the right-hand-man and left-hand-man in unison.

"Then our job," continued The Boss, "is making sure that those 86,400 seconds each day are spent on not just doing things right, or doing the right things right, but doing *only* the right things and doing them right. Why? *Because we don't have time to be doing anything we don't have to do.*"

"That makes sense, I suppose," said the left-hand-man, "but six years ago we had a competitive threat from another company. We focused on Quality, and we've done well."

"We turned things around," added the left-hand-man. "Got back on top. Won Quality awards. Talked Quality. Lived Quality. Breathed, ate, and slept Quality."

"So are you saying now that Quality is not

important?" questioned the left-hand-man.

"That now we focus on time and forget about Quality?" questioned the right-hand-man.

"No, no, no, no, oh my, no, no, no," responded The Boss. "But if there's one thing we know, it's that this moment in time is not the same as this *next* one. Nor were either of those the same as the one we had a few moments ago, or an hour ago, or will have six months from now."

"But what does all this have to do with the plans we developed?" asked the left-hand-man. "How does time apply to those?"

"Very directly," answered The Boss. "You proposed a way to recruit new people. But that's not our problem. Our people are good. We're just not using them as well as we could. Their roles are too narrowly defined. Their tasks are too rigid. We need to cross-train the people we have, not find new ones. And redesign the work flow to be more flexible and adaptable."

The left-hand-man nodded glumly. The right-hand-man took up the challenge. "Are you saying that improving the new product development process doesn't add value?" he asked.

"No, I'm not," responded The Boss. "But all of those rigid protocols and signoffs would have added time. And somehow, *adding* time to a *new* product development process doesn't add up to an improvement to me. If it takes us one year to get out a product, and the marketplace is changing every six months, well, that seems like a problem to me."

"But what about consolidating our edge based on price?" the left-hand-man asked.

"Of course a price advantage is important," responded The Boss. "But if we set up our policies, practices, protocols, and processes primarily to pursue price, but don't have what customers want when they want it, I don't see that as much of an edge. Do you?"

"No," mumbled the right-hand-man.

"I guess not," added the left-hand-man, shrugging.

The Boss was beginning to get a bit exasperated. He anticipated some resistance, but he didn't think it would be this strong. So he decided to play his ace in the hole.

"Look!" he said, more than a wee bit louder. "Don't you find it interesting that EMIT, Inc., comes out with new products and services, and in the time it takes for us to come up with a plan to deal with them, they've come up with still *newer* products and services? Well, *don't you?*"

At this, the right-hand-man and left-hand-man sat up straight. There was something in The Boss's tone, a level of authority that out-Bossed The Boss.

"How did you do that?" asked the right-hand-man.

"Yeah," added the left-hand-man. "That last thing you said. It sounded 51 percent like a question and 49 percent like an exclamation. How'd you do that?"

The Boss smiled and pulled a ‽ out of his pocket for the right-hand-man and left-hand-man to see. "It's called a Question Point. Guess who makes it?"

They didn't need to guess.

"But how do you know it hasn't been on their drawing boards for years?" challenged the right-hand-man. "How can you be so sure EMIT, Inc., turned the idea into a product so quickly?"

"Because ," smiled The Boss, "I had my daughter-in-law phone them with the suggestion yesterday, via their 800 line."

"But yesterday was a holiday," said the skeptical left-hand-man.

"I know," said The Boss. "That's why, when my daughter-in-law received the express delivery of free Question Points as a thank-you for giving them the new product idea, there was a note apologizing for having taken so long to get back to her."

The right-hand-man and the left-hand-man nodded. But The Boss still wasn't sure they truly understood. So he pressed on.

"I see things differently now," The Boss said. "I look at inventory and I think in terms of the time it took to make it—and will take to sell it.

"I look at our people, and I think of the time it takes to train them—or to recruit and hire them in the first place.

"I look at paperwork, and I think of the time it took to generate—and the time it will take others to respond to it.

"What finally dawned on me is that, in the final analysis, we have just one resource. Our time. And our success *does* hinge on Quality—the quality of the way we use that time."

He sat back to gauge their reaction. Truth be told, The Boss was quite discouraged. He had made what he thought to be his strongest case, and his right-hand-man and left-hand-man were still not fully persuaded.

I've thrown everything at them but the kitchen sink, and they still don't get it, he thought.

And just then a fortunate thing happened. Thinking about the proverbial kitchen sink made him think about his own kitchen.

And thinking about his own kitchen made him think about breakfast.

And thinking about breakfast made him think about last night's breakfast nightmare.

And thinking about last night's breakfast nightmare made him think about teaspoon cleaners, and Kitty Kat, Kitty Kat, and back-ordered corn flakes and bananas.

And so he began to explain about teaspoon cleaners and Kitty Kat, Kitty Kat, and back-ordered corn flakes and bananas to his left-hand-man and right-hand-man.

He told them the whole story. When he had finished, the three of them sat in silence for several moments. The Boss wasn't sure whether this was good or bad.

The right-hand-man was first to break the silence. ·

"Are you done?" he asked.

"Yes," said The Boss.

The left-hand-man added, "Do you have anything else to say?"

"No," said The Boss, more concerned than ever. Were they still unconvinced?

The right-hand-man and left-hand-man looked at each other, with smiles playing at the corners of their eyes. Then they turned to The Boss and spoke in unison: "It's about *time!*"

For just a brief instant, The Boss was taken aback. Had all this precious time been wasted? Were they being insubordinate? Impertinent?

Then he saw the broad grins on their faces, and he knew he had in fact gotten through.

It's about time? Indeed it is, he thought, very, very, happily.

EIGHT

It had been about a year since the feisty reporter from the *Gazette* had visited The Boss.

In that time, Punctuation, Inc., had turned back the threat of EMIT, Inc.

There was a good story in this, and the *Gazette* reporter, being a good reporter, was out to get it. (And being feisty, he was out to get it first.)

The Boss, his left-hand-man, and his right-hand-man greeted him at Punctuation, Inc.'s main entrance.

"Welcome," said The Boss, with the right-hand-man's and left-hand-man's nods silently echoing the greeting.

"Yeah, yeah, hi," said the *Gazette* reporter. "Long time no see. What's all this?"

He barreled past the Punctuation, Inc., three-some and approached a lobby display of the products and services that had been most responsible for the company's victory over EMIT, Inc.

- Teethers—Punctuation, Inc.'s response to Gurglers. (These had a vitamin-enriched material to help in tooth and gum development. In record time, Punctuation, Inc.'s now time-conscious legal staff had been able to turn back regulatory-based objections driven by the powerful periodontist lobby.)

- Hum-Babes!—body-language punctuation marks to be used in baseball games by third-base coaches.

- Syntax Seminars—a series of pro bono courses offered at area high schools to help kids improve their written and verbal communications.

"More than any other products," The Boss explained, "these helped us turn things around when EMIT, Inc., began to turn up the heat."

"Oh," said the *Gazette* reporter, scribbling furiously. Noticing this, the left-hand-man proffered a small plastic package.

"What's this?" asked the *Gazette* reporter.

"A new product," answered the left-hand-man. "We call them Notables. They're for people who need to take a lot of notes in a short amount of time."

The reporter looked suspicious. "You're not trying to buy a good story by giving me freebies, are you?"

"If it will make you feel better," said the right-hand-man, "you can pay us for them."

The reporter looked horrified.

"He's just kidding," The Boss reassured him. "Of course you don't have to pay. And of course we aren't trying to buy you off. Just trying to be helpful. But if you'd rather not accept them . . ."

"No, no, no," responded the reporter, quickly. "They're fine. Thanks. I was just a little concerned."

"Understood," said The Boss.

Trying to recover his composure, the *Gazette* reporter looked around the lobby area and framed a new question.

"If you're making so many new products," the reporter continued, "where are you making them?

This place looks the same size as it was a year ago. I want to see your facilities. All that extra capacity. All that extra floor space."

"But you're looking at our facilities," said the right-hand-man. "The bigger the buildings, the farther things have to travel. The farther things have to travel, the more time it takes to make them. And we can't afford to waste all that time since time is, after all, money."

The reporter noted this in his notebook using his Notable. Then he posed another question.

"To make the kind of sophisticated advances you've made, you must have hired more sophisticated workers . . . more sophisticated job descriptions . . . a higher degree of specialization. Can I see those job descriptions? Can I talk to some of those new workers?"

"You're welcome to talk to whomever you want to talk to," responded the left-hand-man. "And you can feel free to peruse our job descriptions. But I think you'll be kind of surprised."

"How so?"

"Because the workers are the same ones who were here a year ago," continued the left-hand-man. "And if anything, the jobs are less specialized. Too much specialization doesn't make sense. It's like having one person wash just the teaspoons after dinner."

The reporter looked confused, The Boss bemused.

"We want people to be able to do what needs doing, when it needs doing," The Boss explained. "Flexibility is the key to *real* productivity."

By now they had moved through the lobby out to the factory. The Boss pointed out the factory floor and said, "Maybe this will give you a better picture of what we've been talking about."

What the *Gazette* reporter saw was rather remarkable. Because instead of the traditional assembly line, the work was being performed in small, U-shaped work cells. Instead of each worker performing a single task over and over and over and over and over and over and over again, each worker performed a variety of tasks, moving to where he or she was needed, doing what needed to be done.

As the reporter was taking all this in, a bell sounded in the work cell and all the workers in the cell looked up at a message board. The board had a number of columns with permanent headings: PRODUCT, MODEL, QUANTITY. When the bell rang, the spaces under the headings were filled in with the appropriate information. Once the workers saw the information, they went to work, filling the order.

"What was that bell?" asked the reporter. "Where did that signal come from?"

"It means we got an order," said The Boss. "Paperwork takes time, and we don't have time for a lot of it around here, so we post the order as soon as we get it. Then we get to work building it as soon as it's posted. We figure that if we build things as people buy them, there's less chance that we'll be building things no one wants to buy."

The reporter thought about the sensibility of that statement.

"Of course," added the right-hand-man, "this system is still too slow for us."

"Too slow?" challenged the reporter. "You've got people working on the order seconds after it comes in, and you call that too slow?"

"Time is money," said the left-hand-man. "We get the order in the sales department, and then we post it. That's an extra administrative step that doesn't really add any value. We're working on bringing our customers directly on line so they can enter orders directly. Speed things up."

The reporter shook his head, amazed and skeptical. "OK, OK, OK," he said. "All that new stuff is kind of interesting. But let's get back to the basics. You've got all these new products. I'd like to see your warehouses. You must be doing some interesting things there."

"Warehouses?" asked the right-hand-man.

"Yeah, warehouses!" answered the reporter, feistily. "You know . . . where you keep all your inventory."

"Inventory?" asked the left-hand-man.

The Boss could see that the reporter was confused (and getting a little exasperated), so he jumped in.

"You're looking at our inventory," The Boss said, gesturing to the factory floor. "Since we build to order, we don't have any, except for work in process. And we'd like to drive that to zero."

"But if you don't carry any inventory, how do you respond to customer needs?" asked the reporter.

"Quickly," answered The Boss, semifacetiously. "We used to think that carrying a lot of inventory helped us be responsive. But all that inventory lengthens the pipeline between us and our customers, and that's not good for anyone. We'd wind up spending time trying to persuade customers to buy what we had, rather than figuring out ways to build what customers need."

"You wouldn't go to a restaurant for breakfast if you had to take what they had decided to prepare that day, would you?" asked the right-hand-man. "If, say, you wanted corn flakes and bananas but all they had was French toast?"

Once again the reporter was confused; once again, The Boss bemused. "Carrying no inventory gives us a wonderful incentive to figure out ways to streamline the production process," The Boss said.

The reporter was intrigued. Skeptical, but intrigued.

"But what about Quality problems?" he asked. "Wouldn't they be a disaster for you?"

"Oh, absolutely," said the left-hand-man.

"Unmitigated," said the right-hand-man.

"Then," pressed the reporter, "how do you deal with Quality problems?"

"We deal with them," said The Boss, "by working like crazy to make sure we don't have any. Because we can't afford to have them, we make sure that we don't. That we do it right the first time."

The *Gazette* reporter made a Notable note that that word "time" kept cropping up in this story.

"Rework takes time," continued The Boss, "and time is money."

"But every now and then, *something* must go wrong," said the reporter. "People are, after all, only human. Mistakes do happen."

"True enough," said The Boss. "That gives us another advantage."

The reporter was incredulous. "How?"

"When we make a mistake," explained the left-hand-man, "there's no safety net. As soon as we make it, we find out about it. Our customers are very good at letting us know."

"And that's an advantage?"

"Absolutely," said The Boss. "Or at least it's a whole lot better than putting that mistake on a shelf in a warehouse and continuing to make that same mistake until one of those time bombs gets into a customer's hands. By then, we might have thousands of bad products that we have to scrap. Thousands of customers in for an unpleasant surprise. And who knows if we'll ever be able to trace the root cause of the problem at that point. The trail is pretty cold by then."

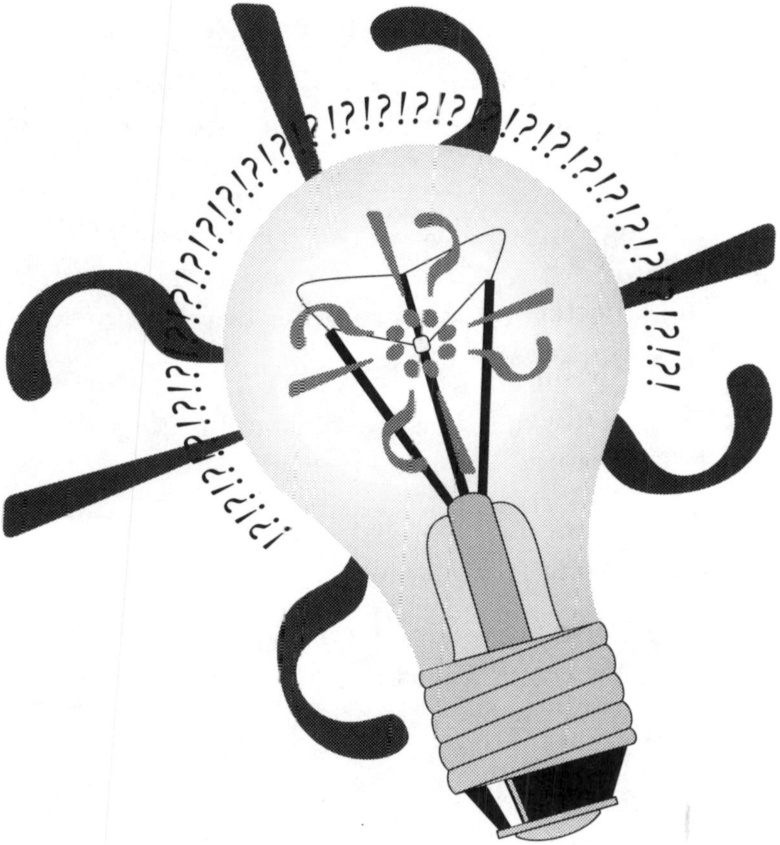

The reporter was beginning to get the picture. "So," he said, uncharacteristically tentatively, "being able to shorten the time it takes for problems to get to customers is an advantage?"

"In a strange way, yes," said The Boss. "More important, it's a terrific incentive to make sure that we don't create any problems that can get out to customers."

The reporter took a deep breath as he made more notes. Although he thought he was getting it, he again decided to take a breather by returning to safe, orthodox, business stuff.

"So," he asked, "what are you running this week?"

"Excuse me?" responded The Boss, the left-hand-man, and the right-hand-man.

"You know," explained the reporter. "To fill capacity. You can't afford to have idle capacity."

"Well," said The Boss, "we'd certainly rather not have capacity just sitting around. But we don't build to forecast. We decided that predicting what customers would buy from us so that we could gear up a lumbering process to produce what customers probably would want six months from now wouldn't add as much value as creating a process that was fast enough to produce what customers know they want when they want it. We wait until we get an order—"

Suddenly a bell rang in the work cell below them. The workers looked at the message board above, and got to work.

". . . and then we build it. That way, customers are pulling it from us, rather than us pushing it on them. Seems to work better."

"What about new product development?" asked the reporter. "How does that fit into this approach?"

"It's critical," said The Boss. "And a real challenge. Demands are so great, it's hard to keep up. We've been getting better at it, though, since we've been through twenty-three new product development cycles in the past week."

"Twenty-three in one week!" exclaimed the *Gazette* reporter. "I can see where getting through that process sooner would be a big edge."

"It is," said the right-hand-man. "But it's not just that we can get done with a new product development sooner. It's that we can start on it later."

"Huh?" asked the reporter.

The left-hand-man came to his rescue. "It's amazing how much smarter you can be when you're trying to anticipate what customers might want tomorrow instead of what they'll want next year."

The reporter seemed perplexed and a little frustrated.

"Is something the matter?" asked The Boss, solicitously.

"Yes. I mean no. I mean, I'm having a hard time communicating my point," the reporter tried to explain. "I think I see what you're saying. I think I'm excited by it. But I can't find a way to get that across. I'm not sure if it's a question or a statement. Probably 51 percent a statement, 49 percent a question."

Hmmm, thought The Boss. He made a quick note and handed it to the right-hand-man. The right-hand-man read the note, nodded, excused himself, and headed off down the hallway. He returned thirty seconds later.

During that half-minute, the reporter continued to try (unsuccessfully, as it happens) to explain to The Boss and the left-hand-man what he was getting at. His frustration was mounting when the order bell sounded at the neighboring work cell. The words "Exclamation Curve," "Standard," and "One" went up on the production board under PRODUCT, MODEL, and QUANTITY. Thirty seconds after that, a worker from the cell walked over and handed The Boss something that looked like this:

‽

The boss then handed it on to the reporter and said, "Here, try this out."

The reporter seemed more frustrated than ever. "I think I understand what you are doing here," he said, "but can't you see that it goes against much of the business orthodoxy‽"

The reporter paused. And then he laughed. Because his last statement had captured his thoughts and feelings exactly and precisely.

"How did I do that?" he asked.

"What you were struggling with was the fact that you wanted to ask a question, but the question was more of a statement than anything else. That's what gave me the idea for the Exclamation Curve you just used. It's our twenty-fourth new product this week. Sorry it took so long to get to you." The Boss turned to his right-hand-man and left-hand-man and said, "We really have to do something about that production board. Much too slow." (There wasn't a hint of irony in The Boss's voice.)

The reporter was pleased and excited.

"Why don't you tell us about the idea you've just had?" asked the Boss.

"Well," began the reporter. But then he stopped. "How did you know I just had an idea?"

"Because of that," said The Boss, pointing above the reporter's head.

The "that" The Boss was referring to was a little light bulb, like the kind you see in cartoons.

"It's one of the ways we've speeded up the development process," said the left-hand-man. "There are sensors located throughout the building to help us signal when people come up with ideas. Ideas are perishable. We don't want them sitting on the shelf any more than we want product inventory on the shelf. We don't want people to have to go through a cumbersome bureaucratic process, either. I mean if kids had to worry about that sort of thing, they'd never come up with games like Kitty Kat, Kitty Kat, now would they?"

"Of course not!" responded the reporter, getting caught up in the left-hand-man's zeal even though he hadn't a clue what the left-hand-man was talking about.

"So," smiled The Boss, "what is the big idea you've just had?"

"Well," the reporter explained, "I was just thinking . . . it would be great if this Exclamation Curve were adjustable. So I could say something that was 51 percent statement and 49 percent question, or 83 percent statement and 17 percent question, or 64 percent statement and 36 percent question. Am I making sense?"

The Boss looked at his left-hand-man and his right-hand-man. Then he looked at the reporter and smiled. "Twenty-five," he said. "And, of course, you'll get a royalty."

The reporter beamed. "I think I've got it," he said, "but I need a wrapup. Our readers like advice. They like to know how-to. What would you tell them?"

"I'd tell them, 'If you can't measure it, you can't manage it,'" The Boss began. "But the key is in knowing just what 'it' to measure.

"Things like efficiency and productivity? Absolutely essential. But they're dependent variables. The one independent variable is time. Take time out of all processes—manufacturing processes, service processes, and administrative processes—and the rest will follow. Take inventory out of processes and the pipeline will shorten and things will move *faster* and the rest will follow.

"Remember a few basic principles:

1.) Time is the most precious commodity. Each moment is unique and unrecoverable. And that's true in the boardroom, or on the factory floor, or in the office, or in our private lives.

2.) Delivering value to customers is what business is ultimately about, and the thing customers value most is time. Cost is a function of time: 'I could have done it sooner, but it would have cost too much.' Functionality is a function of time: 'We could have had a more robust product, but it would have taken too long.' Reliability is a function of time: 'I need a product that won't break because I don't have time to bring it in for service.'

3.) Don't build rigid, inflexible processes and then try to create a demand for what you predicted customers would want. Build flexible, fast-on-their-feet processes that are able to respond to customer demands as they want them.

4.) Look at all your processes and vigilantly eliminate any steps which do not add value for the customers, which don't enable you

to be responsive, which don't enable you to customize to individual customer needs.

5.) Don't say: 'We need to run high volumes because setups take so long.' Say: 'How can we shorten setups so we can run in batches of one?'

6.) Don't say: 'We need to have safety stock and rework loops and extra inspection to protect our customers.' The only things such practices protect are problems; they insulate problems from solutions. Say instead: 'How can we streamline and tighten our processes so that we won't need safety stock and rework loops and extra inspections?'

7.) Realize that all you have is your time. And victory will go to whoever uses that time the best."

The Boss stopped and asked the reporter, "Does that give you what you need?"

The reporter smiled and said, "Absolutely. There's just one more thing, though."

"Which is?" asked The Boss.

"The name of your company," said the *Gazette* reporter. "You might say that punctuation is your business. But words are my business, and I don't think that Punctuation, Inc., adequately captures what you're all about. After all, those—he pointed to the several light bulbs that were constantly popping on and off over people's heads all around them—aren't, strictly speaking, punctuation marks. And when customers hear your name, they ought to know something about you they didn't know before. Added information that will save them time, that would add more value."

The Boss nodded. "I think you're onto something," he said. "We'll give it serious thought at our next management meeting. Thanks for your insight."

"You're welcome," said the reporter. "The only other thing we have to discuss is that I'd appreciate it if I could run the draft version of my article by you for fact-checking. I don't particularly want a lot of editorializing from you. First amendment, and all that stuff."

"Be happy to," said the left-hand-man.

"How long before you'll have that draft done?" asked the right-hand-man.

"Oh, a week. Maybe ten days," said the reporter.

And although the right-hand-man and left-hand-man were amazed that *anything* could take that long, they were polite enough not to say so to the reporter.

"No problem at all," said The Boss. "Just send it on over to us, and we'll turn it around ASAP."

"Somehow I thought you might," said the reporter.

And at that, all three laughed.

It had been three days since the *Gazette* reporter had visited Punctuation, Inc. And although he had said that the draft would take a week to ten days to complete, he had surprised himself and gotten it done earlier that day.

One hour after faxing the manuscript to The Boss, the reporter received a package. It contained the draft article he had sent. There were no marks on it, other than a note from The Boss, which read: "Looks fine as is. Nice job! I thought you might be interested in the enclosed envelope as well."

Sure enough, an envelope was clipped to the article. Amazingly, it contained a royalty check for the adjustable Exclamation Curves the company had sold over the previous forty-eight hours.

But even more amazing than that was the logo that appeared on the check. Instead of Punctuation, Inc., it now read Punctuality, Inc.

The reporter noticed a postscript to The Boss's note. "P. S.: Your idea for a name change was a good one. We approved it three full days ago, but the people who print our checks and letterheads still don't get it. It took them thirty-six hours to turn it around!"

The reporter smiled. Then he got a mischievous idea. (Were he sitting in a Punctuality, Inc., office, a light bulb would have appeared over his head.) He picked up the phone and made a call.

"Hi!" said The Boss, when he recognized his caller's voice.

"I just got the package you sent me, and I noticed you changed your company's name as I suggested," said the reporter. "And I've got just one thing to say to you."

"And that is?" asked The Boss.

"It's about time!" said the reporter.

"Indeed it is," said The Boss, chuckling. "Indeed it is."

And at that instant, The Boss knew that the reporter understood that:

Punctuality, Inc.

Punctuality, Inc.

The Reporter GAZETTE

Quality is the answer to What.

Customer is the answer to Why.

Time is the answer to How.

EPILOGUE

When it all hit the fan, all this Quality stuff,

Having just done "your best" was no longer enough.

All our attitudes shifted, it seems, overnight

To a widespread requirement to "Just do it right!"

Could we all learn to work to a new paradigm

Once our goals changed again: "Do it right the first time!"?

Moving then to a focus on "Right things done right!"

Else you'd fade, we were told, from the customer's sight.

So we heard the wise words, understood what they meant,

And avoided the trap of becoming content.

For the goal changed again as our defect rates fell

To "Do quality work like a bat outta"—well,

Even though you might think that this must be the end,

Realize a new challenge is round the next bend.

The right answer is "time" when the question is "How?"

It will force the right issue, the focus, the *now*.

Maybe all will see time as the key to the race . . .

Except then something else will emerge in time's place.